WITHOUT MUD, THERE IS NO POTTERY

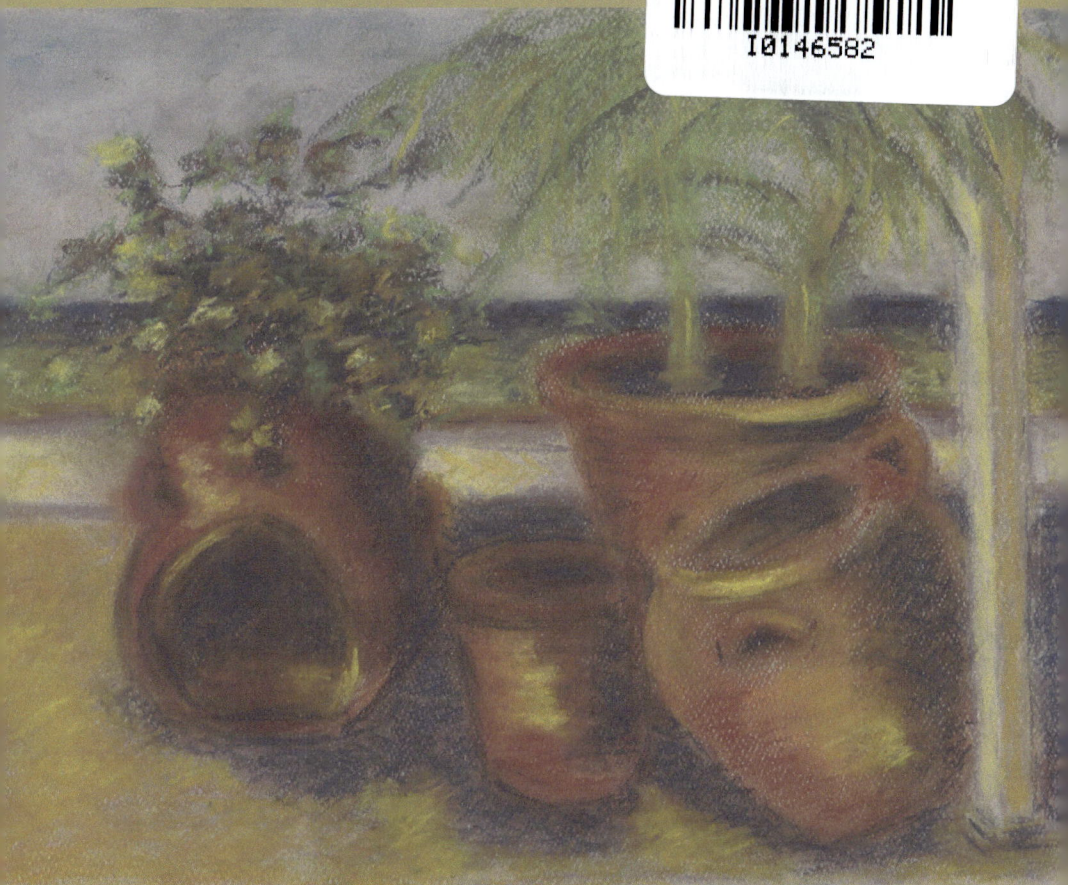

New
Poems By
BILLIE BYRON BENTON

SeaGrove Press
638 Sunset Blvd
Cape May, New Jersey 08204
seagrovepress@gmail.com

DEDICATION

For Margaret
Your pottery graces our home with utility and beauty. Your
love nourishes and supports the soulful life we share.

ACKNOWLEDGMENTS

My forever gratitude to the many clients I have counseled over forty plus years. They have taught me valuable lessons and enriched my life.

When I sit with a client, we walk together, hand in hand, into the deep waters of our human condition. I am challenged to look at my own life, to proceed with diligent care, truth and compassion, so that when I fall, I will pick myself up with the same courage as my companion.

Ronald Thomas Rollet, my publisher and friend, for his vision, support and promptings, without whom this book and others I have written would not have been born or published.

Lu Ann Daniels, for her artist's eye and skillful work in photographing my paintings for this book.

Books By This Author

Without Mud, There Is No Pottery

Stolen Time

Still Here: Prayers For The Living

Here, Then Gone

Love Songs To Margaret

There And Back Again: The Art of Billie Byron Benton

Our Family Garden: Poems, Paintings and Other Art Work, by Billie Byron Benton & Margaret Heritage Perryman & Lori Benton-Janetta

Singing A New Song

Without Mud, There Is No Pottery
and all of Billie Byron Benton's books are available on Amazon.com, local bookstores, from SeaGrove Press, and from the author:
PO Box 93, Mays Landing, NJ 08330

TABLE OF CONTENTS

FORWARD
MY SILENT CHILDREN   i
  BY MARGARET HERITAGE PERRYMAN

POTTER'S HANDS #1   1
A PICNIC LUNCH   2
GIVE THANKS   4
BROCADE   6
ROSES AND THORNS   7
THE POTTER'S WHEEL   8
SEEING DIFFERENTLY   11

POTTER'S HANDS #2   12
TODAY   13
WHAT JUST HAPPENED?   14
THE SOUL SPACE   16
LOVE SONGS TO MARGARET
       VALENTINE'S DAY 2020
       THE SPACE BETWEEN   17
       CELEBRATION   18
WINGS UNSEEN   22
DARK AND LIGHT   23
POTTER'S HANDS #3   24
FLOWERS OR NOT   25
TWO FAWNS   27
SWIMMING   28
BEAUTY   29
EIGHTY-FIVE-YEAR-OLD'S DIARY   31
MANY PARTS   32
BROKEN BOWL?   33
POTTER'S HANDS #4   34
OVERHEARD   35
IN THE DEPTHS OF COBALT BLUE   40
THE MIRROR   42
LIFE UNTIL…   43
POTTER'S HANDS #5   46

TABLE OF CONTENTS

A MYSTERY   47
SOMETIMES   48
FAIR WEATHER AND FOUL   49
BODY AND SOUL   52
POTTER'S HANDS #6   53
LIFE OUTSIDE EDEN   55
A MEDITATION   57
POTTER'S HANDS #7   58
ON WISDOM   59

POET'S BIOGRAPHY   63

PAINTINGS

ROOFTOPS	*FORWARD*
RECITAL	*5*
SOMBER SILENCE	*10*
BLUE MAN	*15*
ATLANTIC CITY JAZZ BAND	*20–21*
I'M HERE	*26*
JUST YOU AND ME	*30*
REVERIE	*38–39*
THE MESSAGE	*44–45*
JIM AND ESSIE	*50–51*
EYES THAT SEE	*54*
FRIENDS THROUGH THE YEARS	*58–59*

FORWARD

MY SILENT CHILDREN

Oh, shapes of earth, formed not of my womb, but of
my hands, sliding wetly through soft fingers, open palms;

Fingers pressed gently toward, seeking to feel each
other through muddy walls slowly rising;

Fingers seeking to guide out the lumps and
imperfections, just as any mother would.

Oh, dried sand, handled with the delicacy of
newborn babes, that the slightest wrong touch,

too heavy or too harsh will damage you forever beyond
repair, like a child whose parent is too rough with her.

Oh, adolescent bisques, that await the final
mother touches if you are to fully become;

The dippings and brushings, with learnings you
and mother alike cannot foresee, only hoping that
the fires of life will inure and forge your true colors;

Accepting that neither can say or know what the
finished being will be, will see, will do.

Oh, my silent children, children of my heart and
hands, children who do not laugh, yet do not cry;

Sons and daughters aplenty but no Mother's Day hugs,
no grandchildren but my children just the same;

Babes, teens, and adults who will live beyond my years,
an assortment of unworded messengers that say I was
here and it mattered to them.

Margaret Heritage Perryman

POTTER'S HANDS #1

She digs clay in river banks
and lake beds, a meditation,

approaching the sedimentary soil,
open to possibilities breathing within.

Strata of mud deposited over millennia,
silently singing it's arias of beauty

to be released, aesthetic pieces of
pottery to be created, everyday

vessels to be formed. All waiting
awakening in her shovels of clay,
dug one after the other.

A PICNIC LUNCH

During the Covid-19 viral pandemic,
my wife and I do our part,

spending most of our time at home
observing social distance,

she, sewing protective masks
for our family and others,

still seeing clients in
sanitized space, talking

with others on the phone
or connecting on zoom,

soothing their fears,
quieting their anxiety.

I, in turn, talk with
clients on the phone,

both of us safe, each
on an end of the line.

Then there are the times
we take a picnic lunch
and find a scenic vista.

This time, a small park beside
the Maurice River, bathed in

sun, lighting marsh reeds
on the opposite shore,

the singing of sea birds
in our ears, wind blowing

across the bay, up the river against
our bodies and into our souls.

Having eaten our lunch, refreshed
by sun, wind and water,

we put the bones of our meal
in a bag and prepare to leave.

Pausing, we look up and notice
our national flag at half mast,

remembering those felled by
this deadly virus,

bodies and bones resting
in their own burial garb.

Tears of grief and the immense relief
of still being alive fill us as we drive away.

GIVE THANKS

When you see and your eyes
sparkle or tear, celebrate!

When you hear and your
belly quakes, rejoice!

When sweet or pungent aroma
fills your nostrils, enjoy!

When you taste and your
mouth dances, give thanks!

When your body is in pleasure,
know you are still alive and real!

GIVE THANKS!

AMEN! HO! SO BE IT!

BROCADE

As the dusk of evening filters through
windows, I look across the living room.

My empty chair is poised, waiting for
its owner. Years of sunlight has

danced through window panes on
flowered brocade, now faded and

threadbare, this beloved chair, a
gift from a friend so long ago.

How fitting, eldering chair, aging
man. Each molded to the other,

tattered and torn, knowing they
are right on schedule, timing

perfect, creaking here, sagging there,
each affirming and comforting the other,

no untoward demands, each
celebrating this time of life.

ROSES AND THORNS

A rose between thorns
doth grow,

as a prick of pain and drops
of blood make clear

and without the thorns,
roses would not appear.

THE POTTER'S WHEEL

"No, not that part of me.
You can't see this.

You might leave,
I'm so ashamed."

"Oh, my beloved,
Come, sit with me.

Be close. Be near,
your head on my lap,
hearing my lullaby of love.

We are clay together,
You and I.

Mud and diamonds intermixed,
clay and emeralds interspersed,

Pearls surrounding,
abundant as the stars,

shimmery as the sun,
all the more lustrous
for their earthy settings.

All are there, gems prized
for their beauty and value.

Earth, lowly, yet mother of
life, fertile in birth.

Share and I will share in return,
as together, we offer ourselves

to the potter's wheel, to be
shaped into useful vessels,

each with its own distinct perfectly
imperfect flaws and markings.

SEEING DIFFERENTLY

Perhaps it is seeing differently
what is already here,

that broken is also whole,
that what we need to learn

we already know, that the
peace we seek is in our

next breath, even though
strife is all around.

POTTER'S HANDS #2

Clay of the potter's hands
and clay of the river bank

blends together, each needed
for mud to become pottery.

Clay she dug from below top
soil, soaks in water,

becoming thin enough to pass
through a sieve. Her hands

pick out rocks, pebbles and
other impurities. Time now

for silence of sun and waves of
wind to dry the mixture to a
workable consistency.

TODAY

TODAY IS NOT A DAY TO THINK
IT IS A DAY TO DISCOVER.

DISCOVER TODAY, THINKING
WILL FOLLOW!

AMEN! HO! SO BE IT!

WHAT JUST HAPPENED?

He was asked to poke the sapling
into the earth, one of many

to make a sweat lodge. He
poked again and again.

The earth deflected each attempt.
I looked on with interest, surprised
he would even try.

Then, following instructions,
he thanked Mother Earth for

her gracious bounty and asked
her to receive the sapling for
the sacred ceremony.

Once again, he pushed the sapling,
seeking an opening.

This time, Mother Earth opened,
the sapling entering with ease,
standing upright,

ready to join the other branches,
to be bent and woven together,

providing a domed space for
the heat and sweat.

He thanked Mother Earth
for her kindness.

I, being both the doer and
observer, am amazed by
this mysterious experience

and wait for the hot coals
to be ready.

THE SOUL SPACE

I GO DOWN TO THE SOUL SPACE SEEKING,
WONDERING WHAT WILL APPEAR,

ONLY TO FIND THE SOUL ALREADY
HERE IN THE PLACES I DAILY INHABIT.

AMEN! HO! SO BE IT!

LOVE SONGS TO MARGARET

VALENTINE'S DAY 2020

THE SPACE BETWEEN

Dear Margaret,

There is space between
that separates, yet joins,

blessing both your life
and mine, as together we
journey these many years.

Space that allows our souls
to seek their own truth

and being, even while affirming
the path of the other.

With magnetic force the space
between binds us together, so strong
is such acceptance and love.

Love,
Bill

LOVE SONGS TO MARGARET

CELEBRATION

Dear Margaret,

HERE YOU ARE, MY
LOVE, SEVENTY-FIVE.

How, when, where, who knows,
but here, now, nevertheless.

And if you were not here now,
where would you be?

I shudder to think, for undoubtedly
it would be without me.

A thought I cannot entertain,
for to do so causes me pain,

not for me alone, but for hundreds,
perhaps, even a thousand or more,

teens you have sheltered,
children you have aided in adoption,

staff needing to find their own strength
and talents while being members of a team,

clients and others you have mentored
and taught, loved and affirmed,

helping them to rise from depression,
and quiet their anxieties and fears.

Imagine the ripple effect to others who have
benefited from those you have touched.

Healing coming through your soul to souls
open to receive and then shared on and on...

Margaret, I celebrate the gift of you, born June 18,
1945.

Love always,
Bill

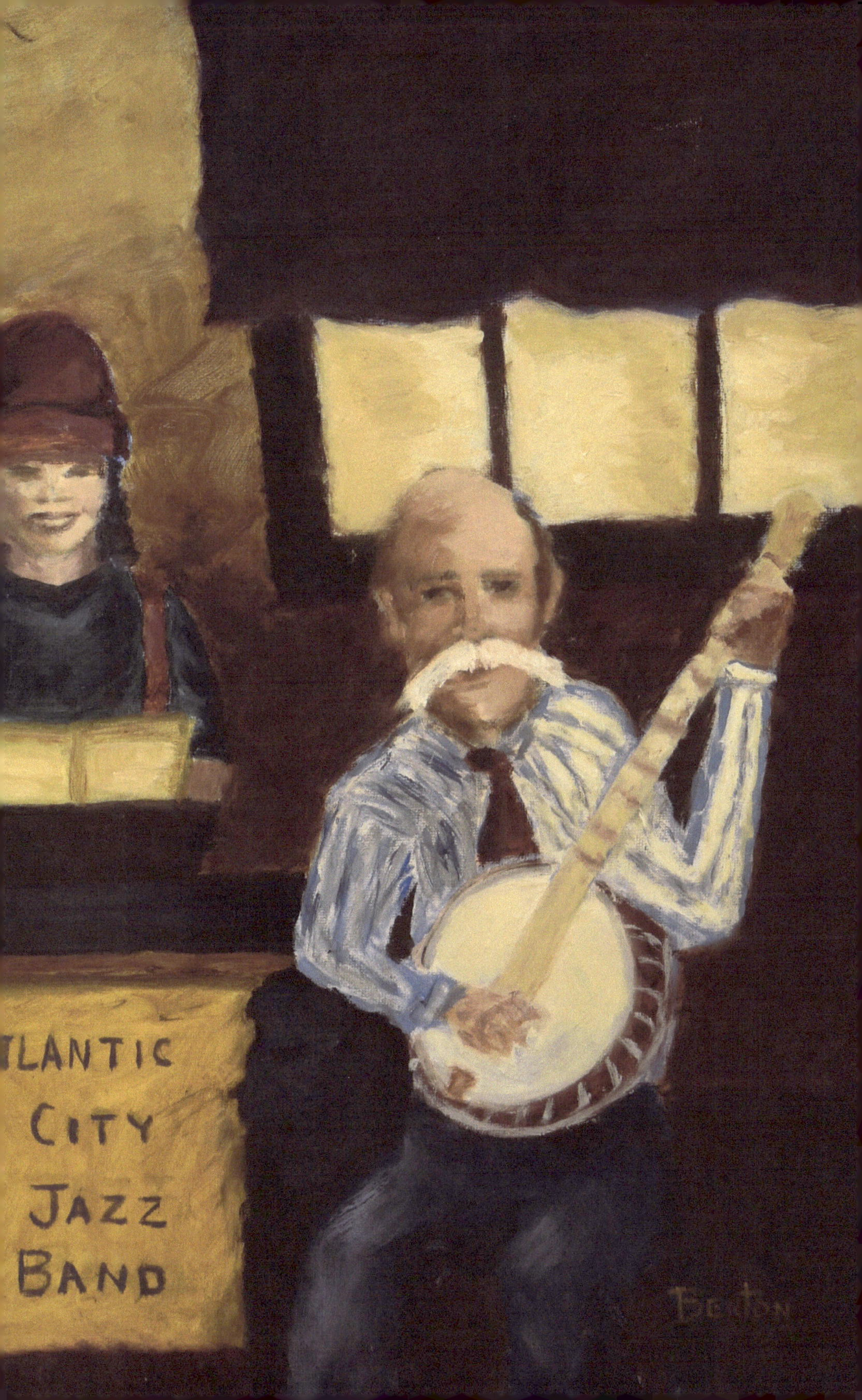
LANTIC
CITY
JAZZ
BAND

WINGS UNSEEN

The years fly by unbidden
on wings unseen,

yet all to obvious,
even if hidden.

Then, of a sudden,
undeniably there,

playing hide and seek still,
one day strong and able,
the next, almost weak and feeble.

DARK AND LIGHT

At times, life's dark storms overwhelm
and heart breaking tears tumble down,

then later, the sun cracks through
and, once again, the warmth of
your smile lights the way.

POTTER'S HANDS #3

Potter's hands and eyes,
seeing and feeling clay

from the river bank, waits,
seeking just the right mixture
of mud and water to appear.

The form of what she will fashion
begins to make itself visible.

Excitement grows. The itch to
create stronger and stronger.

And first, the clay calling,
needing to be kneaded.

Working the block of clay
back and forth as if it were

bread dough, she presses hard
to push out air bubbles, so that

the resulting piece of pottery
will be solid, strong and stable.

When she is finished, she puts
the clay aside. Tomorrow she

she will slice off enough for the
piece she has envisioned.

FLOWERS OR NOT

Looking out the window
on this frigid February day,

trees bending to gusts of wind blowing,
sun bright with cold winter's light.

A flash of brilliant blue catches my eye,
an empty, barren urn, soil frozen,

no flowers in sight, awaiting fresh
planting, come spring's delight.

Will these old fingers and bones also
bend to sift and fertilize, once days
lengthen and warmth returns again?

A question that awaits its own answer,
peonies, mums, and forget-me-nots,
invisible now, beckon and call.

What will we see, come April and May?
Let us then revisit that flash of blue and see.

BENTON

TWO FAWNS

Two fawns lightly leap
in our garden keep,

floating freely, as if unhampered
by weight and gravity.

Innocent and curious assuming
safety their guarantee,

two ballet dancers bending
to graze and explore.

Children at play, unaware
of the two mastiffs on
guard in the neighboring yard.

We hope that Eden will
prevail for yet another while.

SWIMMING

TO MAKE DISCOVERIES IS TO
SWIM IN THE SEA OF UNKNOWING.

HAVE YOU HAD YOUR SWIM
YET TODAY?

BEAUTY

Once I saw a drawing of a hag.
My friend looking on

perceived a beautiful woman.
We argued, each claiming to

be right, sweating and swearing
until each saw as the other.

Beauty all around, unseen until it
becomes visible to eyes looking on.

BENTON

EIGHTY-FIVE-YEAR-OLD'S DIARY

Up at 8:30am
Jury-rigged repair for ancient flip phone

Ate breakfast
Showered, brushed teeth, shaved, toileted

Laid down on floor, slowly
Stretched arms, legs, neck, back

Accomplished 100 ab crunches and
10 push-ups. Stood up even more
Slowly, using bed as a support

Congratulated myself
Laid down on bed
Took a nap

MANY PARTS

THERE ARE MANY PARTS TO US,
ALL VITAL, ALL IMPORTANT.

THE MIND CHEWS ON FACTS,
THE HEART IS NOURISHESD BY COMPASSION.

AMEN! HO! SO BE IT!.

BROKEN BOWL?

THE BOWL ON MY DESK WITH A PIECE
OUT OF ITS SIDE IS BROKEN POTTERY.

THE MOLE ON A STARLET'S FACE
IS HER BEAUTY MARK.

I WONDER WHAT MAKES THE DIFFERENCE?

POTTER'S HANDS #4

A serviceable, yet aesthetically pleasing
bowl of medium size for the family table.
A bowl to be used. Pottery to be treasured.

Last night she had dreamed of this bowl
sitting in the middle of the table,

varied colors dipped, dripped and painted
inside and out, glazes sparkling in reflected

light, heaping full of a favorite vegetable,
fresh from the garden.

Now, she slices off a chunk of clay, molding it
around the center of the wheel, wetting

her hands with watery clay slip. She turns
the wheel on, resting her hands softly around
the clay, feeling it slide wetly through her fingers.

In meditative stillness, she gently slows
her breath, noticing each inhale and exhale,

grounding and centering, becoming solidly
present, inhabiting both body and soul,

with the felt sense of uniting with the clay,
clay of soil into clay of humanity.

Then putting pressure with the heel of her
hands, the clay centers.

OVERHEARD

OCCASION: Picnic Lunch
SETTING: Banks of the Maurice River
TIME: Two months into Covid-19 Pandemic
CIRCUMSTANCES: Most businesses, organizations and
                   services closed, except those deemed
                   essential, citizens ordered to stay home,
                   to go out only when needed, to wear a
                   protective mask when out, and to keep
                   a safe distance of six feet from others.
WEATHER: First sunny day in two weeks

"I had to get out!'
"Yeah, me too!"

"Went down to put my boat in,
thirty to forty people there,

standing around, close together,
no one wearing a mask. I left."

"They just don't get it, do they?"
"Yeah, the new normal."

"Other night we got take out
from the Olive Garden.

Love their shrimp scampi,
delicious sauce. Bite size
asparagus, not over done."

"Can't wait til my wife gets back
to teaching, You know, the honey

do list, the yard, the garden, a new
deck. I'm exhausted"

"I'm looking for a therapist, my
mother, she's so anxious, in her

seventies, scared. Its this virus
thing. A week ago we had to

take her to ER, a panic attack.
They prescribed Xanax and
Lexapro. Not help much yet"

"They just opened the golf course,
my buddy couldn't get a tee time,

the sixty and seventy year olds
had it all booked."
"No, already. Ya gotta by kiddin"

"So that's your new rod and reel?"
"Yep, my goal was a fifty footer,

mounted, but they they just took
it off the list. Somebody landed one."

"How you doing?"
"We buried my son last week."

"I'm so sorry to hear that"
"The rest of us tested negative."

"Mommy! Mommy! That man
just caught a fish! Can I go see it?"

"Ok with me, ask him."

"Mr., can I see the fish? What
kind is it?"

"Sure, come on over. Its a perch"

"Can I touch it?"

"Sure, here, I have it off the hook.
Put your fingers, like this, on either
side of his head. Here, hold it tight.
Would you like to take it home?
It's good to eat. Ask your mother."

"Mommy, can I?"

"Yes, Danny"

"Here, you hold it like I showed
you. Carry it over, put it in your
bucket of water."

"Oh, thanks Mr."

"You're welcome. It'll taste good tonight."

As we left our picnic area on the banks
of the Maurice River,

I noticed our national flag, tattered,
hanging limp at half mast.

IN THE DEPTHS OF COBALT BLUE

I look into his eyes of cobalt blue,
the haunted shadows gone,

there is a strong pull to stay
and sail on the surface,

scanning near and far horizons,
whatever may appear.

At times two dimensions seem
safer than three.

Yet there is a force drawing me
deeper, deeper and deeper still.

The cobalt blue invites me
into into its depths,

with each fathom of descent,
there is an excitement of discovery,

yet dread is also swimming here,
deeper, deeper and deeper still.

Universal opposites appear,
at first slowly, a few gliding by.

Not disturbed by each others' presence,
then more and more, faster and faster,

war, peace; love, hate; birth, death;
male, female; gay, straight; young, old;

black, white; rich, poor and on and on,
seemingly endless.

"No! No! Take them away, I say.
I need to retreat to the surface."

Yet deeper, deeper and deeper still,
until my belly feels peace begin to grow.

Opposites, all a part of the whole,
so hard to contain them all,

often in conflict, each seeking to win,
only to kill and be killed again and again.

They are all here in the cobalt blue,
each a mirror for the other,

all a part of the whole, going
deeper, deeper and deeper still.

THE MIRROR

YOU LOOK IN THE MIRROR, THERE
YOU ARE, THE KEEPER OF THE KEY.

THE KEY, WHAT KEY?

YOU KNOW, THE KEY TO YOUR LIFE.

BUT...

THE CHOICE IS YOURS.

BE WHO YOU ARE.
DO WHAT YOU DO.
HAVE WHAT YOU HAVE,

OR RUN AND HIDE IN THE LAND
WHERE NO MIRRORS RESIDE.

LIFE UNTIL…

When the sun comes down
like rain and tears flow like a river,

your heart breaking like a shattered mirror,
are there any shards left to piece together or is all
lost and left to the ash heap of deadened dreams?

Hear the cry of life shouting your name, lifting
the bloodied shards from still hot coals,

awaiting your determined will to fashion the
new mosaic and to live, live, live until the

pieces have found their final form
and the great AMEN is heard at last.

AMEN! HO! SO BE IT!

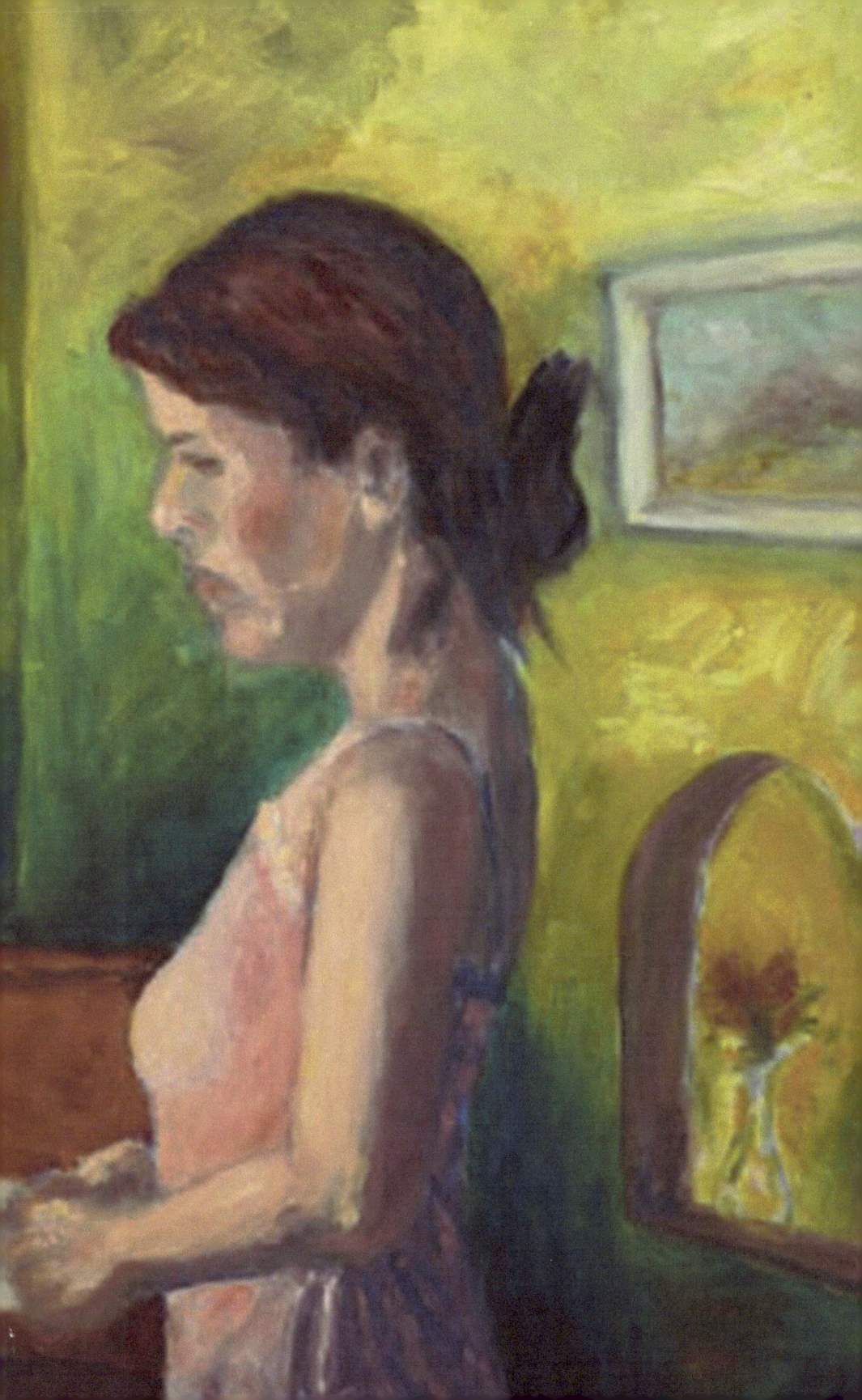

POTTER'S HANDS #5

After centering the clay with heel of her
hands, she puts her thumbs together and pushes
down and apart, forming the base of the bowl.

Now, the sides. Taking more watery slip, she
places her hands together, one inside and one out,

drawing her fingers up slowly, gently,
almost touching, with slippery clay between.
She continues until fingers sense the desired
thinness reached.

This accomplished, she loosens the bowl
from the wheel with a slicing wire and
moves it to a plaster bat to dry.

When dry enough, she gently carries the bowl
to the wheel, placing it upside down in the center,

held in place with rolled up pieces of raw clay.
Using a carving tool with the wheel moving

slowly, she carves the bottom, leaving a rim
of clay around the base of the bowl.

She moves the bowl to the bat and sets it aside
to dry the rest of the way, ready for bisque firing.

A MYSTERY

A summer's dream, humid air, thick
with wetness, intense furnace hot sun

waves landing, one upon another,
dragging Eddy and Billy into slow
motion, Sunday afternoon, nothing to do.

Their preteen voices cracking as they
spoke softly, hushed by heat and humidity.

Without a plan, arriving at Eddy's house,
they sought shade at its side.

Sultry winds blew curtains through an
open window. Drawn by some unseen
force, they crept closer.

Eyes agog, they saw Eddy's mother and
father laying on their bed napping,

yet, not exactly sleeping. Intrigued,
with stirrings in their bodies, not yet

understood, they watched Eddy's
mother, clad in a see-through slip,

climb atop his father, begin to
sway back and forth in slow motion,
making soft, sighing sounds.

Hearts pounding, with strange sensations
in their genitals, they scrambled away.

Without a word, they parted, going
their separate ways.

Each to discover, in their own time, the
sublimely physical and sacred mystery
they had just seen.

SOMETIMES

Sometimes there is no answer
to the why behind our tears.

There is only what is, at that moment,
darkness and rending pain.

And the SUN will continue to rise,
DAY will inexorably follow night
and LIGHT fill our sight.

FAIR WEATHER AND FOUL

Trees breathing in the wind,
tossed as fresh blown waves,
forty feet from tip to trough.

Clouds sailing from branch
to branch, tree to tree,

charting their own course with-
out regard to magnetic north.

The blue of the sky and the sea
meeting in constant embrace,

faithful to each other in fair
weather and foul, treading
a path sought by lovers all,

bending in the wind,
weathering the storms
and staying the course.

BODY AND SOUL

So, there's the list, the
always and everlasting list.

Bending high, towering low,
there wherever we go

and if not done, there will
be hell to pay, for the un-
done will there, forever lay.

On the other hand, the soul
doth dance its inviting tango,

seductive in its call to seek
the intangible, for that which

is most worthwhile is often
not achievable, yet is most

important for fullness of life,
otherwise, we are untethered

with no compass in sight,
bound to sail the surface

hither and yon, victims of gentle
and hurricane winds blowing

us to tropical paradise or to
tsunami sacrifice.

Perhaps, the mundane and the
holy need to be wed into some

spontaneous whole, inhabited
by both body and soul.

POTTER'S HANDS #6

She prepares glazes for the bowl cooled
from bisque firing,

Choosing favorite recipes, a clear glaze, an earthen
brown, and a cobalt blue, she mixes them, one
by one, pouring their powder into water and stirring.

She pours clear glaze into the bowl, turning it
around quickly, draining the excess out.

She then coats the outside, holding it upside
down, dipping the bowl up to the foot.

After the clear glaze has dried, she drips
the earthen brown and then the cobalt blue,

inside and outside of the bowl, letting them
find their own patterns and shapes, running
together and apart as they may.

Eagerly awaiting the glaze firing, she remembers the
dream of the serving bowl and senses that this is it.

LIFE OUTSIDE EDEN

White policeman's knee on black man's neck,
"I can't breathe!"

Knee stays on neck.
"Ma Ma help! I can't breathe!"

More than eight minutes later, no
more words, no more breath, only silence.

George Floyd is dead.
A match is struck to the tinder of racism.

Outrage, heartbreak,
the volcanic red lava of loss and

and rage over centuries erupts.
Protests sweep like wild fire

through city after city.
Many peaceful, others become
violent, destructive, even deadly.

President Trump fanning the flames.
"Call up the National Guard.

Stop the violence of lowlifes and losers.
If there is looting there will be shooting."

Pocked marked store fronts, smashed windows,
looted stores, buildings a fire, burned out cars.

Banners, people marching, chanting for
an end to police brutality, and racism,
calling for justice and equality.

Ten-year-old white child, "I'm here so
black people won't die for no reason."

Another voice, "This is the beginning of
the end of something...It has to be..."

A county prosecutor, "We have to talk with
our white counter parts. We have to become
allies in how we change this problem."

George Floyd's brother pleads for peace.

Nashville, more than sixty National Guard put
down their riot shields at the request of protesters.

Beaufort, police and protesters march together and have a
barbecue following the march, black and white together.

In other cites, some white police and black protesters
embrace, seeing the hurt and need in the others' eyes.

Are the gates of Eden in sight?
A plea, that no matter what, we use

our life's breath to move in that direction,
to make this mud into pottery.

A MEDITATION

Letting your awareness wander
to your breath, gently notice

the natural rhythm of the
inhale followed by the exhale,
automatically, in breath following out breath.

There will be a pace, a cadence that
is uniquely yours. Just spend a few

moments noticing and enjoying
the wonder of it all, anchoring

your attention to the way your breath
effortlessly gives you the gift of life.

Then begin to say to yourself, as you breathe,

> "Inhale peace, exhale love.
>   Inhale calm, exhale compassion.
>
>   Inhale peace, exhale love.
>   Inhale calm, exhale compassion.
>
>   Inhale peace, exhale love.
>   Inhale calm, exhale compassion.

Saying these words four or five times,
you will notice a calming, a centering

within and an opening outward to others.
Repeat as wished.

POTTER'S HANDS # 7

Having made enough pottery for a glaze firing,
she prepares the kiln, coating the shelves to

prevent pieces from sticking, arranging them
in the pattern and heights needed.

She begins loading the kiln, placing each
piece in place, stopping to lay a firing cone

on the heating unit and when ready closes
the lid and starts the kiln. Eight hours later the
heating cone has melted and the kiln turns off.

Twelve hours after, the kiln is cool enough
and she opens it. It feels like Christmas.

She gazes at the bowl, her favorite piece,
its shapely form and brilliant colors.

Then, she glances at the gray block of clay
from the river bank and marvels at the
miracle, once again, mud has become pottery!

ON WISDOM

The Spirit Guide arrived in the village square.
People gathered to hear his words.

"Master, speak to us of wisdom."

"Wisdom is in your tears and laughter,
your joy and sorrow.

Time is the great revealer, allowing the
fruits of life to blossom, to grow, and ripen.

Wisdom requires you to become a receptive
student, whether in pain or in bliss,

to cross rivers that come along, through storms
that beset, being tested again and again,

becoming stronger with each lesson,
soul expanding and deepening.

Each of you have your own journey,
your own wisdom to discover and
universal truths to experience.

You are all part of humanity, joined
inexorably together, that includes

the good, the bad and in between,
all found within each.

Acceptance, compassion and love
for self and others are necessary,
as well as safety and protection.

There will be a deepening of joy
as the adventure continues.

You are both the mud and the potter.
It is wise to create attractive and useful
pottery for the good of all."

With these words the Master ended his teaching.

All were together in silence.

BIOGRAPHY

Bill, christened Billie Byron Benton, received his BA in philosophy from the University of California at Berkeley, his MDIV from Union Theological Seminary in New York City, and his MSW from Rutgers University of New Jersey. Bill has worked as a Presbyterian minister, a social worker, and a psychotherapist.

Bill has published several books both of poetry and art.

Bill and Margaret, his wife, partner, and soul mate, reside in Southern New Jersey where Bill has been writing poetry and winning awards for his oil paintings for many years.

www.ingramcontent.com/pod-product-compliance
Lightning Source LLC
Chambersburg PA
CBHW041357090426
42739CB00001B/7